# When You're Sick or in the Hospital

## Healing Help for Kids

Written by
Tom McGrath

Illustrated by
R. W. Alley

ONE
CARING
PLACE

Abbey Press
St. Meinrad, IN 47577

*In gratitude for all the courageous pediatric nurses*
*who hold the children in their care so tenderly in their hearts.*
*And especially for the angelic nurse so long ago who shared some 7-Up*
*and comfort when I was a sick and sad and scared little boy.*

Text © 2002 Tom McGrath
Illustrations © 2002 St. Meinrad Archabbey
Published by One Caring Place
Abbey Press
St. Meinrad, Indiana 47577

Library of Congress Catalog Number
2002103655

ISBN 0-87029-367-2

Printed in the United States of America

# A Message to Parents, Teachers, and Other Caring Adults

Illness is scary for any of us, but it can be especially disturbing for children. Illness is an assault on one's very person. It can leave a child feeling confused, afraid, and possibly even guilty. Those who are ill often also become disconnected from normal life, friendships, and interaction with the community. The sick child can feel very abandoned and alone.

Children need caring adults to help them navigate their way through illness, medical treatment, or a stay in the hospital. They will undergo procedures that they may not fully understand. These tests and treatments, though necessary and good, may be painful and demanding. The medical personnel who treat your child may be experts in their field, but they certainly are not experts on your child's temperament, feelings, and fears.

Try to be an advocate and trusted companion for your child. You have the opportunity to accompany her through the process of treatment and care, to explain as honestly as you can, to be present as much as you can, to reassure in whatever ways you can, and to find ways to help her stay connected to normal life as much as possible.

As adults caring for a sick child, we need to deal with our own anxiety in order to be truly present to the child. When a child feels bad, it hurts those of us who love him to see him going through such agony. It's important to avoid the twin temptations of either turning to mush or turning to stone. Or, worse, turning and fleeing the scene.

You can be a "bridge over troubled water" for a sick child, a soothing presence, a source of confidence, and a connection to normal life. I hope that reading this book together will help you and the special child in your life to navigate your way through this time of illness with comfort, hope, and healing.

—*Tom McGrath*

## Being Sick Is No Fun

When you are sick, your body feels bad. You may not feel like doing the things you usually do. You might need to have medical tests, get shots, or take icky medicine. You may have to stay in the hospital for a while.

Nobody wants to be sick. It's okay to be mad about it—or sad or scared. It helps if you know a few things about being sick, and about your sickness. It helps to understand why you feel bad and what you can do to get better.

Remember, there are many people who love and care about you. They want to do everything they can to see that you get well.

## Life Is Different

When you're sick, your life changes. You might not be able to run and play as you usually do. Sometimes you can't hang out with your friends. You may have to miss baseball games or a party.

If you stay in the hospital, you will be sleeping in a different place and eating different kinds of food. You might share a room with someone you don't know.

A hospital can be busy and noisy and sometimes even scary. Even though a hospital can seem very strange, everything that happens there is meant to help you get better.

# It's Okay to Be Mad or Sad

Being sick can make you grumpy or mad. Sometimes you feel lonely and sad. And often you just feel bad.

It's normal to having feelings like this when you're sick. As you get better, you will feel more like yourself again. Your life will become more like the way it was.

Tell your feelings to someone who understands, like your parents, or the nurse, or your aunt when she comes to visit you.

## Ask Questions

You probably don't know why you feel bad. You might wonder what's going to happen to you.

Ask the doctor, nurse, or your parents anything you want to know, like:

Why do I have to take that medicine?
Why do I need to stay in bed?
When can I get up and play again?

Sometimes the grown-ups you ask won't know all the answers. Ask anyway, so that the people taking care of you know what's on your mind.

# Stay Connected

When you're sick or in the hospital, you can't be with your family and friends as much as usual. This can make you feel lonely.

Even though they can't be with you, your family and friends still love you and care about you. Keep something close to you that reminds you of your home and family—like a favorite stuffed animal, or a family picture, or a scarf that smells like your mom's perfume.

When I was seven years old and sick in the hospital, my classmates wrote me letters and drew pictures for me. This helped me to feel connected with my friends. I still have that box of letters today! See if your friends can send you some letters or pictures.

# Don't Blame Yourself

No one wants to get sick or to get hurt. You try to take good care of yourself, so you can stay healthy. You try to play safely, so you won't get hurt.

But sometimes people do get sick or hurt. Maybe you caught a bad germ. Maybe you had an accident. Maybe something in your body just isn't working right.

This is not a time to blame yourself for being sick or hurt. Your sickness is not a punishment for doing something wrong.

This is a time to think about what you can do now to feel better. That means listening to the doctors and others who care for you and following their orders.

# If You're Afraid, Say So

Being sick and getting medical treatments can be scary. So don't be surprised if you feel afraid.

The best thing to do when you feel afraid is to say it out loud. Then it's not a secret anymore.

The grown-ups who care for you can help you not to feel so scared. They might hold your hand, or talk to you to take your mind off being scared. Just feeling calmer can help your body feel better.

# When It Hurts

Sometimes what the doctors do to help you feel better can feel really bad at first. But everything they do is to make you feel better.

Getting a shot isn't fun, for example, but it may be the best way to get the medicine inside you. The nurses and doctors are not trying to hurt you on purpose. Often they'll let your mom or dad stay with you during the parts that will hurt. It always goes better if you don't put up a fight.

Here's something to think about. When you grow up, maybe you can study really hard and invent an easier, less painful way to help children who are sick.

# Being Scared—and Brave

Think about firefighters, police officers, and others who help people in danger. They often feel afraid. But, even though they are afraid, they are brave, too. They do what they need to do to help others.

Being brave doesn't mean you have no fear. It means you don't let fear stop you from doing what needs to be done.

You are being brave, too, when you do hard things so that you can get better. The people around you are proud of you for being brave.

# Say a Prayer

Many people pray when they are sick or feel all alone. You can pray by yourself or with someone else.

If you're in the hospital, you may get a visit from a "chaplain"—someone who helps people feel closer to God. The chaplain can pray with you, or listen to your questions and feelings.

Some people believe in guardian angels, who stay with us all the time and look out for us. Guardian angels remind us that God is always with us and always cares about us.

If you want, you can pray this little prayer: "God, I don't feel well. Please help me feel better. Stay close to me during my sickness and let me know you always care. Amen."

## Have Some Fun

When you're sick, you can't run outside and play like you normally do. This is not to punish you, but to give your body the chance to get well.

You can still find ways to have fun. Maybe you have a special doll, stuffed animal, or action figure to keep with you and play with. Maybe you have a favorite book or video game to enjoy.

If you're in the hospital, there may be a playroom with toys and games for children who are well enough to play.

# Think Happy

When I was a young boy in the hospital, it was wintertime. Out the window I could see children sledding down a snowy hillside. At first I was sad because I was stuck in bed. But I remembered times when I was making snow forts and sledding down hills, and that made me happy.

If you feel bored or lonely, think about times when you were playing with your friends or at the beach on vacation. Happy thoughts in your mind can help your body to heal.

Think of times when something funny happened in class, or about a movie that brings a smile to your face. If someone is in the room with you, you can tell each other funny stories.

# Tell Your Story

When you're sick or in the hospital, it can seem like so much is happening to you, but you can't do much of anything.

Why not make a scrapbook or journal about your sickness? Or you could make a storybook for other kids telling them what it was like for you. Maybe it will help them to have an easier time when they are sick.

Ask your family to get the supplies you need, and help you to put your book together. It will be something you can keep and feel proud of, long after your sickness is gone.

# Your Bright Spirit

**W**hen you are sick, it can feel as if your whole world is falling apart. You might even start to think that life will never feel good again.

**B**ut there's a part of you, deep inside you, that no sickness can ever touch. It is called your "spirit." It's the part of you that makes you YOU and joins you with God. It's the part of you that makes you strong and brave. It's a golden part of you that will always shine like the sun.

**W**henever you feel your worst, go to this golden place within you. Feel God's love and goodness there. Be well!

**Tom McGrath** is the author of *Stress Therapy* (Abbey Press) and *Raising Faith-Filled Kids: Ordinary Opportunities to Nurture Spirituality at Home* (Loyola Press). He writes the monthly family spirituality newsletter *At Home With Our Faith* for Claretian Publications. Tom is also editorial director for TrueQuest Communications. He and his wife, Kathleen, live in Chicago with their two daughters, Judy and Patti, and their cat, Missy.

**R. W. Alley** is the illustrator for the popular Abbey Press adult series of Elf-help books, as well as an illustrator and writer of children's books. He lives in Barrington, Rhode Island, with his wife, daughter, and son.